REVOLUTION!

REVOLUTION IN EUROPE 1989

Patrick Burke

Thomson Learning
New York

REVOLUTION!

1848: Year of Revolution

The American Revolution

The Easter Rising

The French Revolution

Revolution in Europe 1989

The Russian Revolution

Cover: *Student demonstrations in November 1989, in Czechoslovakia. The demonstrators have cut the Communist symbol out of their flag.*
Title page: *December 23, 1989: A man carrying the Romanian flag—with the Communist symbol cut out—passes an army tank in front of the presidential palace in Bucharest.*
Opposite: *Jubilant East Germans prepare to cross the border between Czechoslovakia and West Germany, November 7, 1989.*

First published in the United States in 1995 by
Thomson Learning
New York, NY

Published simultaneously in Great Britain by Wayland (Publishers) Ltd.

Library of Congress Cataloging-in-Publication Data
Burke, Patrick.
Revolution in Europe 1989 / Patrick Burke.
    p.   cm.—(Revolution!)
  Includes bibliographical references and index.
  Summary: Discusses recent events in Eastern Europe, focusing on the decisive year that saw the fall of Communist governments in several countries.
    ISBN 1-56847-422-9
  1. Europe, Eastern—History—1989– —Juvenile literature.
[1. Europe, Eastern—History—1989– 2. Europe, Eastern—Politics and government—1989–] I. Title. II. Series: Revolution! (Thomson Learning (Firm))
DJK51.B87   1996
947—dc20   95-34777

Printed in Italy

Picture Acknowledgments
The publisher would like to thank the following:
Associated Press/Topham 7, 17, 18, 24, 27, 29, 30, 32, 34, 40, 41; Camera Press 4, 8 (bottom), 9 (bottom), 13 (bottom), 14-15 (bottom), 20, 21, 26 (top), 28, 38, 39; Impact 35 (bottom), 37; Frank Spooner Pictures: *contents page*, 8-9 (top), (top), 19, 22, 26 (bottom); Popperfoto: *title page*, 11, 16, 25, 31, 35 (top), 36, 42, 43; Rex Features 5, 10, 14 (top), 15 (top), 33; Robert Harding Picture Library 44; Tony Stone 6, 23.

CONTENTS

THE BERLIN WALL COMES DOWN

TIME LINE

World War II Nazi Germany invades and occupies Eastern Europe and parts of the Soviet Union.

From 1944 Soviet forces liberate Eastern Europe, then occupy and impose Communist system on each country. Nazi Germany defeated in 1945.

Late 1940s Communists gain full control in Eastern Europe.

1985 Mikhail Gorbachev becomes General Secretary of the Communist Party of the Soviet Union. Begins to develop policy of non-interference in internal affairs of Eastern European countries.

Thursday, November 9, 1989. At the daily press conference in East Berlin, the exhausted and confused East German Communist Party media boss, Günter Schabowski, announces to the world's press: "all East German citizens can now be issued with visas for the purpose of travel or of visiting relatives in the West. This order is to take effect at once."

His announcement is broadcast on East German TV at 7:30 p.m. Soon crowds begin to gather at border crossing points, demanding to be let through. For a short while, the guards keep the barriers down, waiting for instructions from the authorities. They are still under orders to shoot anyone trying to leave East Germany illegally. What should they do? Finally, acting on their own initiative, they lift the barriers and the crowds pour over into West Berlin.

EYEWITNESS

Erich Knorr, an East Berlin engineer, crossed into West Berlin on November 9: "I can't tell you what it meant to us. All these years we'd been bottled up in our little part of Germany, second-class citizens that nobody wanted, in a country most of us didn't really want to be in. I'd been a prisoner, and suddenly I wasn't a prisoner any longer. I could have shouted and sung and waved my arms. I couldn't stop smiling. A girl came up and gave me a kiss, and I thought I was really in heaven."

Above A young Berliner uses hammer and chisel to help destroy the Berlin Wall on November 10. Only hours before he, and those behind him, could have been shot for climbing onto the Wall. Westerners used their side of the Wall as a canvas on which to paint murals and political slogans.

Left A line of East German cars —Trabants and Wartburgs— surrounded by welcoming West Berliners at Checkpoint Charlie on November 10, 1989. Checkpoint Charlie was the most famous crossing point in the Berlin Wall. The Wall split the city and the country in two and was an international symbol of the division of Europe.

A Street Party

The next twenty-four hours sees the largest street party in European history. Tens of thousands of East and West Berliners crowd into the edge of West Berlin and clamber onto the Berlin Wall. Similar scenes are repeated up and down the East German border. In the first forty-eight hours after the announcement, two million East Germans make the journey west.

The politicians are not far behind. On Friday, November 10, West German Chancellor Helmut Kohl and former chancellor Willy Brandt come to West Berlin to celebrate the historic event.

The opening of the internal German border was the beginning of the end for the Communist regime in East Germany and for East Germany itself. It was also the end of the division of Europe and of the Cold War (the state of tense relations between East and West Europe and between the Soviet Union and the United States), which had lasted since the end of World War II.

THE ROAD TO REVOLUTION

Toward the end of the 1980s the Communist regimes of Eastern Europe were facing several crises. The worst crisis was economic. Throughout the region, production was stagnating, and in some countries there were severe food shortages. Overall, in Eastern Europe in 1989 the increase in industrial production was only 0.1 percent, the lowest ever in Communist history.

Poland, Hungary, and Bulgaria had amassed huge debts to Western banks and governments. (They had borrowed money in order to finance economic reforms, but much of it had been wasted.) Romania had paid off its debt by 1989, but only by exporting most of what it produced—90 percent of its food produce, for example—with wretched living conditions for most people as a result.

Czechs line up for bread in Communist Prague. The Communist system was unable to cope with the complicated needs of a modern society. The result was that many goods were not produced or produced only in small quantities—which is why people had to stand in line for basics such as bread and meat.

Falling Standards

As the economy declined in many Eastern European countries, the welfare state, which was meant to protect people, was also falling apart. The proudest boast of Communist regimes had always been that they could offer their people job security, social services, cheap housing, and free health care. This, they argued, was much more important than the so-called freedom of people who lived in the West.

But in Poland, for example, in the mid-1980s, half of the young couples were told they would have to wait for up to fifteen years for an apartment of their own. Polish hospitals were in a terrible state, overcrowded, ill-equipped, and short not just of medicine but of basic supplies (even bandages were being washed for reuse).

The Richer West

The unhappiness people felt at the decline in their standard of living was increased for many when they compared their countries with the West. Poles and Hungarians could travel to the West, although with some difficulty. East Germans could and did watch West German TV. Though their economy and welfare system were stronger than those of most other Communist countries, East Germans always compared themselves with their much richer West German neighbors.

In Bucharest, Romania, a woman cooks a meal on an electric heating element placed on a stone in the kitchen of her apartment. Living standards for Romanians were among the lowest in Europe: standing in line for hours for butter and a piece of meat was an everyday ordeal for most people.

By the 1980s, Eastern European industry had also had a devastating impact on the environment, creating some of the worst pollution in the world. In some areas, notably the region comprising southwestern Poland, northwestern Czechoslovakia, and southeastern East Germany, pollution had produced ecological disaster.

Opposition to Communism

Economic failure, the slow decline of the welfare state, and the destruction of the environment gave rise to widespread popular dissatisfaction throughout the region. It was obvious that the system had failed. Few people in Eastern Europe believed any longer in Communism. Despite this, most people were either too afraid, or just too busy surviving in difficult circumstances, to oppose their regimes openly.

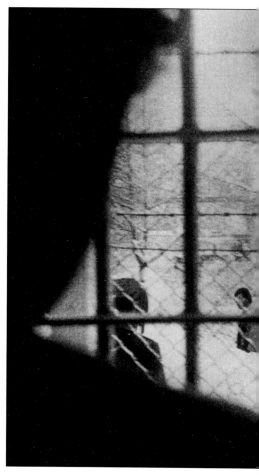

Above A secretly photographed view of Polish dissidents in Bialolenka internment camp after the Polish government's clampdown on the Solidarity movement in December 1981. The Communist government's attempt to crush Solidarity failed, even though it imprisoned thousands of government opponents.

Left Czechoslovak countryside devastated by pollution. In 1983 a secret report by the Czechoslovak Academy of Sciences estimated that in the western half of Czechoslovakia 30 percent of the forests were seriously damaged, 30 percent of all animal life and 50 percent of all plant life were threatened, and 30 percent of all rivers were biologically dead.

However, in every country there were dissidents, people who publicly criticized their regimes and made proposals for reform. Usually gathered together in small groups, dissidents argued that their governments should respect human rights, such as freedom of speech and travel. The dissidents also wanted their governments to pursue more peaceful relations with the West, stop polluting the environment, and introduce economic reforms.

The regimes were afraid of the dissidents, as they knew they were just the tip of the iceberg: the dissidents represented the views of many people, and in some countries even the majority of the population.

Supporting Dissidents

Most dissidents were supported by Western governments, political parties, trade unions, peace groups, and human rights organizations. Because the Communist regimes needed economic help from the West, and wanted to be treated as political equals by Western governments, they usually refrained from subjecting dissidents to the most brutal treatment. Nevertheless, many dissidents lost their jobs, or were imprisoned or forced into exile. Some even died at the hands of the authorities.

In all the Communist countries, dissidents kept the ideas of independence, democracy, and peace alive. In some countries, the fact that the dissidents had been campaigning underground for many years meant they were well organized enough to play leading roles in the revolutions and to ensure that the movements for change had true leadership.

Left *The Berlin Wall, built in 1961, was part of the border built by the East German government to keep its citizens from going to West Germany. The border consisted of a fence or a concrete wall, a mined strip of ground, ditches, barbed wire, self-firing machine guns, electronic warning systems, and watch towers.*

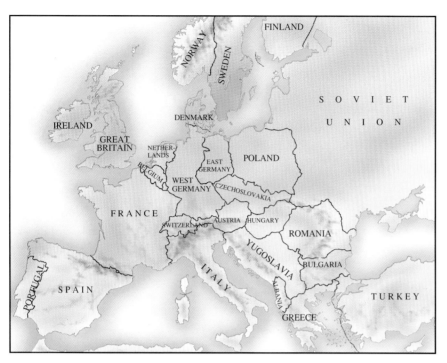

Left *In 1988 all of Eastern Europe was still in the Soviet sphere of influence. The huge armies of the Warsaw Pact and of its Western counterpart, NATO (the North Atlantic Treaty Organization), faced each other in the middle of Europe, armed with thousands of highly destructive conventional, nuclear, and chemical weapons.*

However, neither economic failure nor widespread dissatisfaction with the regime would necessarily have led to the collapse of the Communist regimes. The intervention of Mikhail Gorbachev, the Soviet leader, was decisive. After coming to power in 1985 he began to make it clear that the Soviet Union would no longer use its armed forces to help East European leaders control their populations. This frightened East European leaders: what would they do without Soviet force, or even the threat of it, to back them up against their people?

Gorbachev also introduced political and economic reforms. This not only made it easier for Communist reformers in Eastern Europe to try the same, but also encouraged people who were not dissidents to criticize their regimes publicly. When Gorbachev came to East Berlin in October 1989 crowds chanted "Help us, Gorby!"

By the late 1980s, these pressures had divided the Communist regimes of Eastern Europe into two groups. The Polish and Hungarian regimes realized they would have to introduce fundamental economic reforms. They also understood that economic reform would not work without political change: they would have to cooperate with dissidents and other groups in society whom they had previously tried to suppress or ignore.

Above *Shortly after Mikhail Gorbachev came to power in March 1985, he liberalized the media in a reform known as glasnost, or openness. Perestroika, or restructuring, was the name given to his economic reforms. Gorbachev hoped these reforms would allow the Soviet Communists to stay in power. By December 1991, however, the Communists were out of power, and the Soviet Union no longer existed.*

COMMUNIST RULE IN EASTERN EUROPE

In 1944–45, as it drove back the forces of Nazi Germany, the Soviet Red Army brought Communism to Eastern Europe. The Soviet Union's main concern was to create a band of sympathetic Communist regimes between it and West. By 1948 Europe was divided between the Communist East and the democratic, capitalist West, and Communists were in power in every Eastern European country.

In each Eastern European country, supreme power was concentrated not just in one party, the Communist Party, but in the Politburo of the Communist Party, a body with ten to twenty members, chaired by the Party leader (known as the First Secretary). The decisions of the Politburo were transmitted to society through the Communist Party and other bodies under its control, for example the other political parties, trade unions, and women's organizations. Both government and parliament were run by the Communist Party, which also tried to establish total control of society. No public disagreement with Communist Party rule was allowed.

For many years, however, the peoples of Eastern Europe also enjoyed a reasonable standard of living (although it was much better in some countries, such as Czechoslovakia and Hungary, than in others, such as Romania). This helped to quiet discontent over the lack of freedom. By the end of the 1980s, however, as the Eastern European economies were worsening drastically, this achievement was forgotten.

The second group, East Germany, Czechoslovakia, Bulgaria and Romania—the "Gang of Four"—rejected reform. Their leaders knew that Polish or Hungarian-style economic experiments would require political change, which would destroy them. In any case, the East German and Czechoslovak economies were relatively strong and the regimes could put off introducing reforms. In addition they, and Bulgaria, supplied their people with consumer goods—even if of a low standard—that kept down popular discontent. The Romanian regime, by contrast, starved its population, and its brutal secret police, the Securitate, crushed all opposition.

Above *Infantry of the Soviet Red Army on parade. Some 20 million people—soldiers and civilians— died between June 1941 and May 1945, defending the Soviet Union and pushing the Nazi forces back to Germany.*

POLAND

The collapse of Communism in Eastern Europe began in Poland. This was not just because opposition to Communism had always been strongest in Poland; it was also because, by 1989, the Polish economy was so weak that the regime knew it had to give in to demands for economic and political reform.

Opposition to the regime was spearheaded by Solidarity, the independent trade union led by Lech Walesa, that was founded after national strikes in August 1980. With 12.5 million workers, Solidarity was the largest workers' movement in European history.

Above *Poland in 1989. Poland was independent from other states between 1918 and 1939. Then it was invaded, occupied, and divided up between Nazi Germany and the Soviet Union from 1939 to 1945.*

TIME LINE

1980
Food price rises lead to workers' protests.
August 14: Lenin Shipyard in Gdansk goes on strike.
August 31: Solidarity is founded.

1981
December 12-13: General Wojciech Jaruzelski declares martial law. Solidarity suppressed.

1988
May and August: Workers strike and call for relegalization of Solidarity.
September: Secret negotiations between Solidarity and government begin.

1989
February–April: Round Table discussions among Government, Solidarity, and Roman Catholic church.
June 4: Semi-free elections: Solidarity wins.
August 7: Coalition parties change sides; Solidarity offers to form new coalition government.
August 24: Tadeusz Mazowiecki becomes prime minister.
December 29: The Sejm eliminates leading role of the Communist Party.

1990
December: Lech Walesa elected President of Poland.

LECH WALESA

A captivating orator, Lech Walesa had been a thorn in the side of the authorities since the workers' uprising on the Baltic coast in 1970.

Fired from the Lenin Shipyard in 1976 after an outspoken speech at a meeting of the official union, Walesa, an electrician, continued his dissident activities, helping to set up the Committee of Free Trades Unions. He returned to the shipyard on August 14, 1980 and immediately became the leading figure in the strike, then chairman of Solidarity.

Walesa's cool head and sharp tactics were not only crucial for Solidarity in 1980–81 but also throughout the movement's period of illegality in the 1980s. Having helped Solidarity overthrow the Communists, Walesa was elected President of Poland in 1990.

Lech Walesa (with a mustache) during strikes in the Gdansk shipyards in May 1988.

General Jaruzelski defended the suppression of Solidarity with the argument that it had averted a worse alternative: invasion by the Soviet Union.

Suppressing Discontent

On December 12, 1981 the Polish government, under General Wojciech Jaruzelski, had brutally suppressed Solidarity, arresting tens of thousands of its members and imprisoning Lech Walesa and other leaders. For the next seven years, Solidarity continued to work underground. New unofficial groups emerged and published hundreds of illegal newspapers and magazines.

Between 1982 and 1988, the Jaruzelski government tried to deal with Poland's economic crisis. But the Communist Party had little support in the country, as Poles showed in 1987 by voting against an official economic reform plan.

The breakthrough for the opposition came in May and August 1988, when waves of strikes over price rises and low wages spread across the country. To the surprise of both Solidarity and the authorities, workers raised Solidarity banners and chanted "There's no liberty without Solidarity!"

Left *The Round Table talks. The seating arrangement symbolized that all three groups—government, Solidarity, and the Roman Catholic Church—were taking part as equals. The Communists hoped that they would be able to retain some power. But the semi-free elections in June showed that the Polish people wanted to be free of them.*

Below *A huge Solidarity demonstration on September 17, 1989, the fiftieth anniversary of the Soviet invasion of Poland. Six months earlier such a gathering would have been illegal. In the 1980s Solidarity was an umbrella organization for all Poles who opposed the Communists. After the end of Communism, it split up into competing groups and lost much of its influence.*

After the August strikes, the regime realized Solidarity could not be ignored. For four months it conducted secret negotiations with the trade union. On January 18, 1989, at a stormy meeting of the Central Committee of the Communist Party, General Jaruzelski persuaded the Party to accept the return of Solidarity.

The stage was set for the unprecedented public "Round Table" discussions between the government, Solidarity, and the Roman Catholic church. Never before in Communist Eastern Europe had a Communist regime sat down with its opponents and critics to talk about sharing—or perhaps even handing over—power.

Elections

On April 5, after two months, the Round Table participants signed a historic agreement. The government agreed to legalize Solidarity and recognize the right to strike. Semi-free elections were to be held on June 4 (35 percent of the seats in parliament, the Sejm, were to be freely contested, with the remaining 65 percent reserved for the Communists. In addition a new upper house in parliament, the Senate, would be created; all one hundred seats in it would be openly contested).

The elections were held on June 4, 1989. All but one of the freely contested seats were won by Solidarity candidates. However, the elections results created a new problem, for they left Poland without a workable government. The old-style Communists still had 65 percent of the Sejm seats but no popular support; Solidarity had the support, but no majority in the parliament. In fact, the results were not what Solidarity wanted, as it was unprepared for power.

Above *Pope John Paul II's first visit as Pope to his country, in June 1979, when millions came out to greet him. He was accompanied by Cardinal Stefan Wyszynski.*

THE ROMAN CATHOLIC CHURCH

Of all Eastern European churches under Communism, the Roman Catholic Church in Poland was the largest and most active. In the 19th century, when Poland was partitioned among Prussia, Austria, and Imperial Russia, the Church became a sanctuary of language, culture, and a national sense of Polish identity. In the 1940s and 1950s the Communists realized that they could not suppress the Church, although they did confine the leader of the Church, Cardinal Stefan Wyszynski, to a remote monastery for three years.

After the banning of Solidarity in 1981, the Church stepped in. Priests helped distribute food and clothing sent by Western Church organizations. "We now talk of the 'official' Poland and the 'real' Poland," said Stanislaw Stomma, a dissident in Warsaw. "The place where you find the 'real' Poland is inside the Church." In 1989, the Church played a key role in the Round Table talks that led to the downfall of the Communist government.

Price Rises and Panic Buying

Yet the size of Solidarity's victory meant that a government without its support was unthinkable. The Polish economy was continuing to nosedive: prices shot up after the election and, because they feared further price rises, people indulged in panic buying: the store shelves emptied.

Only a government supported by Solidarity would be strong enough to push through the measures desperately needed to stabilize and restructure the economy. Western governments, too, were saying that they would only provide financial help, which the Polish people so desperately needed, if such a government were in place.

A New Government

Negotiations and maneuvers began over the shape of Poland's new government. First, on July 19, General Jaruzelski was elected President: Solidarity wanted this, as it would guarantee to the Soviet Union that Poland would stay in the Warsaw Pact.

Then Jaruzelski tried to form a Communist-led government with Solidarity as a junior partner, but Lech Walesa refused. Strikers began to demand a Solidarity government: a political general strike seemed to be just around the corner.

On August 7, Lech Walesa invited two small parties to leave the coalition with the Communists and give their support to Solidarity. On August 16 they agreed. Together, these parties and Solidarity controlled 55 percent of the seats in the Sejm. The door was now open to a Solidarity-led government.

Above Crowds fight their way into a butcher shop on July 31, 1989, the day before food prices were expected to rise as part of the government's planned Western-style economic reforms. The reforms brought severe poverty and social insecurity to some Poles.

Right Children join workers in the city of Poznan in 1956 during the Polish uprising against hard-line Communist rule. The flag on the left is stained with the blood of a child killed by government troops. More moderate Communists in power after 1956 failed to introduce the reforms Poland needed: in 1970, the country exploded again, as workers went on strike on the Baltic coast.

OPPOSITION TO COMMUNISM IN POLAND

"The Poles rebel against a mild oppressor, because they can; against a harsh one, because they must." (A Polish saying from the 1860s.)

Opposition to Communism in Eastern Europe was always strongest in Poland. One reason for this was historical. Poles had been rebelling against Russian occupations on and off since the 18th century. When the Red Army imposed Communism on Poland in 1945, many Poles simply regarded this as another example of Russian oppression. At the same time, the Polish Communists had always had only minority support—much less than the Communists of, say, East Germany or Czechoslovakia. Instead,

Poles, whether peasants, workers or intellectuals, remained loyal to the Roman Catholic Church.

Revolts against the Communists broke out in 1956, 1968, 1970, and 1976. Each time the regime was strong enough to suppress the uprising—often using extreme violence and even shooting and killing demonstrators.

In 1980–81, however, Solidarity, was too strong. Only after 15 months, when it was afraid the Soviet Union might invade the country, did the regime try to crush Solidarity. But the fundamental weakness of the regime was obvious, as the events of 1988–89 showed.

The New Prime Minister

Jaruzelski realized he had no choice but to agree to a non-Communist government. Many people expected Walesa to become the new prime minister, but he refused. Instead, Tadeusz Mazowiecki, a 62-year-old Catholic intellectual and adviser to Walesa, was chosen. On August 24 he was elected the first non-Communist prime minister in the history of the Soviet bloc.

For the next three weeks, Mazowiecki worked day and night to put together a new government. On September 12, he presented it to the Sejm. It was dominated by Solidarity but included the Communists and the two smaller parties. In an historic vote, the Sejm voted for it by 402–0, with 13 abstentions. Forty years of Communist rule were formally over.

The Republic of Poland

Within three months the last remains of Communist rule had been swept away. The Sejm voted to remove from the constitution the Party's leading role in government; it restored the country's pre-World War II name, the Republic of Poland; and it returned the traditional crown to the official Polish emblem, the white eagle.

The Solidarity government now faced the enormous tasks not only of strengthening the new democracy but, even more difficult, of creating a strong, successful economy. This task the government started by introducing radical economic reforms on January 1, 1990. Later that year Lech Walesa was elected president of the new Republic of Poland.

Below Solidarity leader Lech Walesa embraces the newly nominated prime minister, Tadeusz Mazowiecki, in Walesa's apartment in Gdansk on August 20, 1989. Exactly nine years earlier in Gdansk, Walesa had been an out-of-work electrician leading a strike and Mazowiecki one of his advisors. No one could have predicted that, within a decade, they would become two of the most influential men in post-Communist Poland.

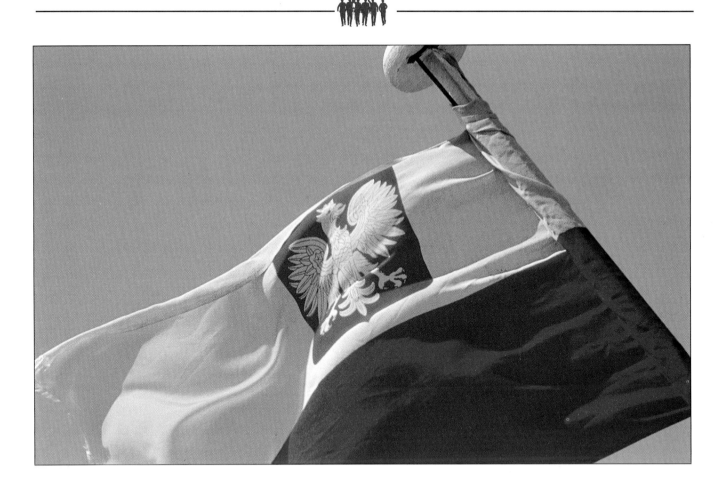

EYEWITNESSES

Magdalena Pawelczyk, 20 years old in 1991, Warsaw: "I do not hesitate to call the years 1989–91 the turning point in our modern history. The times before belong to the past and it seems to me that one day I may forget that I ever lived in a communist country. The young people of Poland have finally reached a time when they can find a purpose in life. We have been given a choice, and a vision of a better future. Western Europe is no longer a forbidden land and the word 'success' has become meaningful."

Striking worker, Lenin shipyard, May 1988, summing up workers' grievances at the constant shortages produced by the "command economy": "Forty years of socialism and there's still no toilet paper!"

Above *The new Polish flag. With the end of Communist rule, the Polish eagle has had its crown restored. The eagle with the crown is a symbol of independent Poland. From the tenth century until it was swallowed up by its neighbors, Russia, Prussia, and Austria, in 1795, Poland was an independent kingdom. Under the Communists, the crown disappeared.*

HUNGARY

In Hungary, as in Poland, the revolution was not a sudden event, but a gradual process of economic and political reform. Here, however, there was no mass movement pushing the regime from below, just a relatively small number of dissidents and other intellectuals. At the same time, within the regime, reformers were introducing change against the opposition of hard-liners.

Both dissidents and Communist reformers knew that the economic system had to be transformed. The dissidents, in addition, wanted to get rid of Communism altogether and introduce a Western-style political and economic system. The Communist reformers accepted the need for political reform, but wanted to ensure that they retained power.

Publishing Attacks

In 1987 dissidents, having gained enough confidence to challenge the regime publicly, published devastating attacks on the government's economic policy as well as demands for political pluralism and a free press. These were followed by the founding of new political opposition groups, including the Hungarian Democratic Forum and the Alliance of Free Democrats.

Meanwhile, at a Party conference in May 1988, reformers replaced Party leader Janos Kadar with Karoly Grosz, and elected a younger, more reformist leadership.

The reformers knew that, unlike the Polish Communist Party, the Hungarian Communists had not lost all support: in free elections, they might have won 30 percent of the vote against the new and inexperienced groups. To make the Party attractive, therefore, reformers began jettisoning as much Communist baggage as possible. By spring 1989, the border with Austria was being dismantled, Kadar had been fired as Party president, and the Party had even announced that Hungary would become a multi-party democracy.

Above *After World War I, Hungary lost more than two-thirds of its lands to other countries, including Romania. The Romanians' bad treatment of Hungarians was a source of tension between the two countries.*

Above *Janos Kadar, Hungary's Communist leader from 1956 to 1988. Kadar enjoyed some support for his more liberal rule, but he lost touch with the people's needs.*

HUNGARY'S PATH AFTER 1956

In October 1956, Hungarians rose up against hard-line Communism and Soviet domination. Thousands died as the revolution was crushed by Soviet tanks. Many more were executed afterward, including the Hungarian leader, Imre Nagy.

Once Communist rule had been firmly re-established, the new leader, Janos Kadar, governed in a relatively liberal manner. His motto was "If you are not against us, you are with us." Over the next thirty years, Hungary became known as the "happiest barracks in the Communist camp."

Up to the late 1980s opposition consisted mainly of the tiny "Democratic Opposition" in Budapest. Liberal and Western-oriented, it defended the principles of free speech and human rights. Its members became leading figures in the Alliance of Free Democrats. By contrast, the founders and supporters of the Hungarian Democratic Forum—known as "populists"—stressed above all "the survival of the Hungarian nation" and focused on social questions such as the falling birthrate and the fate of the Hungarian minority in Romania.

Both opposition groups, the Alliance of Free Democrats and the Hungarian Democratic Forum, drew on the support of the "establishment opposition." These were teachers, journalists, academics, and other professionals who worked with the Kadar regime but remained critical of it. Their main political grievances were the planned construction of the Nagymaros Dam on the Danube, one of the most beautiful spots in a country with few areas of great natural beauty, and the persecution of Hungarians in Romania.

Burned out Russian tanks on the streets of Budapest during the Hungarian revolution, October 1956. The uprising began on October 23, when the secret police fired on a peaceful demonstration. The next day Soviet tanks moved in, but widespread popular resistance forced them to withdraw by October 30. On November 4 they returned in overwhelming numbers and crushed the revolution.

Imre Nagy

But perhaps the most important decision was to allow Imre Nagy, the leader of the 1956 revolution, to be reburied publicly and the revolution to be honored in public. For 31 years after his execution Nagy had lain in an unmarked grave. But on June 16, 1989 250,000 Hungarians gathered in Heroes' Square in Budapest to hear survivors of the revolution call for an end to Communism.

The words of Viktor Orban, a young dissident in his mid-twenties, were cheered the loudest. Standing over Imre Nagy's coffin, he declared: "If we can trust our souls and strength, we can put an end to the Communist dictatorship; if we are determined enough we can force the Party to submit itself to free elections; and if we do not lose sight of the ideals of 1956, then we will be able to elect a government that will start immediate negotiations for the swift withdrawal of Russian troops."

Nagy's reburial was the symbolic climax of the 1989 revolution. By allowing it to take place, the regime was stating publicly not only that the 1956 revolution had been justified, but also that the system that had been installed after the revolution was wrong.

Negotiations

Although the burial of Nagy marked the end of the post-1956 period, the future of Hungary still had to be decided. From June 13 to September 18 the regime and the dissidents negotiated about exactly this. When they finished, they had agreed that Hungary would become a "democratic, independent state," with everyone's rights protected by law.

On October 23, "Republic Day," the new, democratic, Hungarian Republic was proclaimed. Exactly 33 years had passed since the outbreak of the 1956 revolution. The Communist regime struggled on until the democratic elections in March 1990, when they were soundly beaten. Victory went to the Hungarian Democratic Forum which, with the Smallholders Party and the Christian Democrat Party, formed the new government.

Above *The reburial of Imre Nagy, Hungary's prime minster during the 1956 revolution. Nagy supported the revolution's demands.*

TIME LINE

1956
October–November: Hungarian revolution crushed by Soviet tanks. Janos Kadar becomes leader.

1987
September: Hungarian Democratic Forum founded.

1988
May: Janos Kadar ousted as Communist leader. November: Alliance of Free Democrats formed.

Right The view from Buda, over the Danube, to Hungary's parliament building in Pest, the Eastern part of the city. This parliament—Europe's largest—had no proper function under Communist rule: real power lay in the Communist party headquarters nearby. Since 1990 the parliament has played an important part in lawmaking and in the government of Hungary.

1989
June 13: Negotiations between regime and opposition begin.
June 16: Imre Nagy is re-buried
September 18: Opposition-regime negotiations end: far-reaching political and legal changes agreed.
October 23: Republic Day: the new Hungarian Republic is proclaimed.

1990
March: Democratic elections. Hungarian Democratic Forum single largest party.

EYEWITNESS

Eszter Vagi, 18 years old, talking about the past and the present, October 1991: "What did communism mean to us? In political and economic terms it was a failure, a mistake, though the idea is attractive, good but unrealistic. Many issues could not be discussed in the past, or you had just one opinion presented. The good side, in my experience, was that social and material differences were smaller then than now. The whole order of values was clearer. Now it's more confused. Though the multiparty system offers people choice, many people have lost orientation."

EAST GERMANY

In East Germany the regime resisted reform to the end and was toppled by pressure from two directions: from the thousands who turned their back on the country in order to emigrate to West Germany; and from ever larger demonstrations by East Germans who wanted to stay in their country and reform it.

Leaving via Hungary

The emigrants got their first chance in May 1989, when the Communist regime in Hungary began dismantling its barbed wire border with Austria. Suddenly, those who wanted to flee to West Germany were no longer blocked by the internal German border: they could leave via Hungary and Austria. Over the summer, thousands tried to do just that and on September 11, when Hungary fully opened its borders, they poured through Austria into West Germany.

On the same day, however, in East Berlin, dissidents launched a new group, New Forum. New Forum did not call for an end to East Germany or for unification with West Germany; on the contrary, in contrast to the emigrants, its founders appealed to East Germans to take part in a "restructuring of our society."

Above *After unification in October 1990 East Germany became the "five new federal states" in the new Germany. Since that date East Germans have had to get used to a new economic and political system and the disappearance of much of their old way of life. There is some resentment at the West German "takeover" and many East Germans feel that they are treated as second-class citizens.*

Überschreiten der Gleise für Unbefugte verboten

Left *East German refugees arrive at Giessen, West Germany, on October 1, 1989 after an overnight trip from the West German embassy in Prague. In the summer and autumn of 1989 thousands of East Germans occupied West German embassies in Prague and Warsaw until they were allowed to leave for the West.*

EAST GERMANY'S PECULIAR HISTORY

A young East German flees by swimming the icy Tiefersee, a lake on the border between East and West Berlin.

When World War II came to an end, Soviet troops occupied about a fifth of Germany. In 1949, the Soviet Union and the East German Communists established East Germany on that territory. However, many East Germans still wanted a Western standard of living. Between 1949 and 1961, as many as 200,000 people a year left East Germany. After the Communist regime closed the border to West Germany with the Berlin Wall in 1961, the numbers dropped sharply. Many people still applied to leave. Those who tried to escape over the heavily fortified border were shot and killed.

The regime was right to be afraid of reform. In Czechoslovakia, Poland, and Hungary the revolution simply got rid of Communism. In East Germany, the revolution destroyed the country itself: once the Communist regime had been defeated, there was no reason for East Germany to continue to exist as a nation.

Refusal to Reform

But the Communist regime, under the aged and ill Communist Party General Secretary Erich Honecker, resisted all calls for reform or even dialogue. The pressure on the regime did not let up. The weekend of October 6–9 was decisive. On October 7, in East Berlin, during the official celebrations of the 40th anniversary of the founding of East Germany, Soviet leader Mikhail Gorbachev told Honecker in

TIME LINE

1949
October: East Germany (German Democratic Republic) founded.

1989
May: Hungary begins dismantling barbed wire fences along its border with Austria.
August–September: East Germans start emigrating to West Germany through Hungary.
Between August and early October: 30,000 East Germans leave East Germany.
September 11: New Forum is founded.
October: Fortieth anniversary of founding of East Germany.
70,000 demonstrate in Leipzig for reform.
Erich Honecker replaced by Egon Krenz.
November 9: Berlin Wall and rest of East German–West German border opened.
November 10–11: Two million East Germans cross into West Germany.

1990
March 18: "Alliance for Germany" victorious in free elections.

public that "life punishes those who hold back." With this statement he withdrew support from the conservative leadership of East Germany and gave the green light to the younger, more flexible Politburo members.

Two days later, on Monday, October 9, in Leipzig, more than 70,000 demonstrated peacefully for reform. At first it had seemed as if the regime might use the military and the feared and hated security service—the Stasi—against the demonstrators. But, in the end, it decided the risks in using force were too great and the march passed off peacefully. With this decision, the regime surrendered the one weapon it had with which to put down the revolution. From now on, events were driven by the those escaping to the West and by the demonstrators on the streets.

Honecker Deposed

On October 18, Erich Honecker was deposed and replaced by Egon Krenz. Krenz knew he would have to introduce some reforms if the regime was to survive. But he had no credibility: everyone knew that he had not just been a loyal and hard-line Communist all his life, but indeed the Politburo member in charge of the feared and hated Stasi.

Troops of the East German National People's Army march past Party leader Erich Honecker and his regime during the country's 40th anniversary celebrations on October 7, 1989. Within a year East Germany had ceased to exist as a nation.

A massive demonstration in Leipzig on November 18, 1989. Leipzig became known as the "City of Heroes" because of the ever larger demonstrations that took place there every Monday.

The exodus continued: on Krenz's first full day in office, 2000 people traveled west through Hungary.

Meanwhile, the demonstrations got bigger every week. They reached a climax on Saturday, November 4, as almost one million people gathered in East Berlin to demand real reforms in East Germany. This was the largest demonstration in the history of East Germany.

Opening the Border

Then, on November 9, the regime decided to open the border. The decision was an acknowledgment of the anger building up in East Germany over the unfairness of the rules governing permission to visit the West.

Opening the border changed everything. Millions of people traveled to West Germany and saw first-hand how much better the standard of living was than theirs. At the same time their confidence in the Communist regime continued to drop. Two issues in particular angered East Germans: the refusal of the new government to reform the Stasi completely and the evidence that was emerging of the corrupt lifestyle of the Communist leaders: the vacation homes and vacation islands, and, worst of all, the transfer of public funds into private bank accounts in the West.

By the time Egon Krenz succeeded Erich Honecker as Communist party boss, the regime was rapidly losing control of the country. Krenz hoped, in vain, that opening the border would cool protest.

OPPOSITION IN EAST GERMANY

Some East Germans rejected Communism completely and wanted to emigrate to West Germany. Those who did not oppose Communism itself, but wanted to make East Germany more democratic, stayed in the country. From the late 1970s on, more and more such people formed unofficial peace groups that campaigned against nuclear weapons and militarism in East Germany. They also formed human rights, ecology, and women's groups. One of the best-known groups was the Peace and Human Rights Initiative.

The Protestant Church provided all opposition activists with some protection from the regime and allowed them to use rooms and church grounds for meetings and fairs. It was able to do this because it was the only institution that was independent of the regime. Many activists were Christian, though by no means all.

The activists tried to have dialogue with the Communist regime, but the regime treated them as enemies of the state and harassed or imprisoned them.

At the same time, the country was moving closer to economic collapse, as large numbers continued to move West and labor shortages emerged in crucial sectors of the economy. People began to ask themselves what the point was of demanding a reformed and democratic East Germany when, by unifying with West Germany, they could acquire a democratic political system ready-made and enjoy the benefits of joining the strongest economy in Europe.

At the Leipzig demonstrations people began to shout "We are one people!" By this they meant that East and West Germans should have one government. Others simply shouted "Germany, united fatherland!"

Bärbel Bohley and Jens Reich, two of the founding members of New Forum. Bohley, a painter, had been active in opposition circles since the 1970s. As a member of Women for Peace she opposed conscription for women in the early 1980s; later she helped found the opposition group called the Peace and Human Rights Initiative.

The Third Way

Increasingly, opposition groups like New Forum were pushed to one side. These groups wanted East Germany to survive by finding a "third way" between the capitalist West and the Communist East. The outspoken artist Bärbel Bohley, who had been a long-time dissident and a founder of the group New Forum, said, "Being swallowed by the West, that's selling out. We want a democratic socialism." Unfortunately for New Forum, only a minority of East Germans agreed with this view.

Neither the old-style Communist regime nor the opposition could provide the political leadership East Germans wanted. Into this vacuum stepped the West German political parties.

EYEWITNESSES

1990: two different views about the future of East Germany.

W., 18 years old: "I love my country. Formerly I doubted it, but now as I am losing it, I notice how attached I am to it. We are losing a chance which is not likely to recur, to build an alternative to all dictatorial systems (e.g. Stalinism, capitalism)."

An East German worker, February 1990: "People are sick and tired of the 'third way.' Ten out of ten attempts to create socialism have failed. As long as our government has no ideas, people will flock to the West. In one year East Germany can be handed over completely empty."

In January 1990 Prime Minister Hans Modrow set March 18 as the date for democratic elections. The election was only on the surface a contest between East German political parties: the real fight was between the Western parties that stood behind them.

Unification

The central issue in the campaign was, simply, when East and West Germany should unify and under what terms. On March 18, 1990 East Germans voted overwhelmingly for the "Alliance for Germany," the parties linked to the West German government of Chancellor Kohl, because it had promised the speediest possible unification. "Alliance 90," a coalition of opposition groups including New Forum, got a mere 2.9 percent of the vote.

After this, the path to unification was short. On July 1 the economies and currencies of the two Germanies were united. On October 3, full unification of both East and West Germany took place. East Germany, as a separate state, had ceased to exist.

West German chancellor Helmut Kohl waves to supporters in Dresden, East Germany, in December 1989. It was already clear that many East Germans supported unification with their richer western neighbor.

CZECHOSLOVAKIA

In Czechoslovakia, as in East Germany, the regime had to be forced out of power by the people. The first steps were taken by students in the capital, Prague. After a demonstration on November 17, 1989 was brutally crushed by police, the students called a general strike. All workers, not just students, were invited to be part of the protest.

Czechoslovakia was founded in 1918 from some of the provinces of Austria and Hungary.

EYEWITNESS

A woman bystander witnessed the events of November 17: "The police took the people in the first row of demonstrators and beat them mercilessly. They would not let the young people go. They brought in buses and arrested them all."

Martin Polach, a student demonstrator, later said: "You could literally hear the bones cracking."

REPRESSION AND OPPOSITION IN CZECHOSLOVAKIA

In spring 1968, the Czechoslovak Communist Party, under its leader Alexander Dubcek, began to reform the hard-line Communist system. This reforming period was called the "Prague Spring." Almost all Czechoslovaks supported Dubcek's efforts.

On August 21 the armed forces of the Warsaw Pact, led by the Soviet Union, invaded and crushed the Prague Spring. For the next twenty years hard-line Communists ruled Czechoslovakia. Most people criticized the regime only in private. A few dissidents, however, did so publicly. In 1977 a group of them, including the world-famous playwright Vaclav Havel, founded Charter 77.

Charter 77 did not openly oppose Communism; it simply asked the regime to "respect civil and human rights." But the Communists knew that, if they granted these rights, they would not be able to rule. So they persecuted the dissidents, firing them from their jobs, forcing them to leave the country, and, often, imprisoning them. Though small—it only had 1250 members—Charter 77 had great authority. Because of this many "Chartists" were able to play leading roles in the revolution.

Left *Police chase demonstrators in Wenceslas Square, Prague, October 1989.*

The students were quickly joined by existing dissident groups, including Charter 77. Together they formed a new umbrella group, Civic Forum (whose leading figure was the long-time dissident Vaclav Havel) to represent everyone in the Czech lands who supported democratic change. In Slovakia, Public Against Violence played a similar role. Students and dissidents led the revolution, but it was made on the streets, and above all in Wenceslas Square in central Prague. Here, beginning on Saturday, November 18, Czechs gathered every day to hear veteran dissidents, students, actors, priests, and workers demand change.

Left *Alexander Dubcek (holding the flowers) in 1968. Dubcek's popular reforming period was known as the Prague Spring. During the 1989 revolution Dubcek once again became a popular figure.*

Left *Dubcek and dissident leader Vaclav Havel meet just before speaking to more than 250,000 people in Wenceslas Square on November 24. Dubcek is wearing the Czechoslovak national colors in his lapel.*

Right *The day after the resignation of the Communist leadership, half a million people crowd onto the Letna Plain in Prague to hear Dubcek and Civic Forum leaders call for free elections and democratic reform.*

Peaceful Demonstrations

The demonstrations were peaceful, cheerful, and determined. Every day they got larger: and not just in Prague, but throughout the country—in Bratislava, the capital of Slovakia, in Brno, and in Liberec. As the days went by, it was clear that the future of the Communist regime was at stake.

The regime's response was confused. It knew it had little support in the country. When hard-liners tried to mobilize workers against the protesters, they were shouted down. They could not even persuade the security forces to suppress the demonstrations.

The demonstrations reached a climax on Friday, November 24, when Alexander Dubcek, the Communist leader during the Prague Spring of 1968, came to Prague. For over twenty years he had been silenced by the regime. Now, as he stepped out onto a balcony to speak, a huge roar met him. "DUBCEK! DUBCEK!" echoed off the tall houses up and down the long, narrow square. Then he uttered words unthinkable only weeks before: "Dear people of Prague, I am glad to be among you after so long a time." And then: "The light was here before. Why should it be dark again? We had the morning. We must act now as though the light has come once more." As the demonstration ended, the people in the square, in a spontaneous gesture, took keys out of their pockets and

TIME LINE

1948
February: Communists seize power.

1968
Spring: Dubcek's government launches reforms.
August 20–21: Warsaw Pact forces invade Czechoslovakia.

1989
November 17: 20,000-strong student march in Prague violently suppressed by police.
18–19: Protests in Wenceslas Square against the police violence.
19: Civic Forum founded.
20: 200,000 demonstrate in Wenceslas Square for freedom and democracy.

Every night that week, the demonstrations get bigger.
23: Workers pledge support for general strike.
24: Dubcek speaks in Prague. Milos Jakes and the Politburo resign.
25: More than 500,000 demonstrate in Prague.
26: Formal negotiations begin between Prime Minister Adamec and Civic Forum leader Vaclav Havel.
27: General strike
December 10: New government with majority of non-Communists sworn into office.
29: Vaclav Havel elected president.

1990
June: Civic Forum wins democratic elections and forms government.

shook them, 250,000 key rings producing a sound like a mass of Chinese bells.

Defeat

That night, Communist leader Milos Jakes and the entire Politburo admitted defeat and resigned. Civic Forum had scored a decisive victory.

Almost an anticlimax, the general strike the students had called for took place on Monday, November 27. For two hours, the whole nation came to a halt. Even Prague's taxi drivers stopped work, blocking the capital's highway with a two-mile ribbon of cars. Everyone joined the strike; it was, after all, safe to do so. The Communist leadership was near total collapse. During negotiations, the new Communist Party leader, Karel Urbanek, said to Vaclav Havel: "We are aware of the fact that we don't have the trust of the people. We simply lost it—this trust. I say it quite openly." He was right. On December 29, Vaclav Havel was elected President. Communist rule in Czechoslovakia was over.

ROMANIA

Below Romania pursued an independent foreign policy, for example, declining to participate in the Soviet-led invasion of Czechoslovakia in 1968. For this reason, Western leaders ignored Ceausescu's abuses of human rights.

The Romanian dictatorship was overthrown in a quick and violent revolution that claimed the lives not just of hundreds of ordinary people, but of the dictator himself, Nicolai Ceausescu.

The revolution began on December 16, 1989, in the western town of Timisoara, with demonstrations in defense of a pastor who was being persecuted for his criticisms of the regime. When the Army and the feared security service, the Securitate, moved in to put down protests, they killed more than one hundred people.

For four days, the country was quiet. Then, on December 21, anger at Nicolai Ceausescu erupted again. This time, however, to everyone's amazement, it happened in front of his eyes, as he was addressing a staged rally in the capital, Bucharest.

Right Citizens of Timisoara, some carrying the Romanian flag, ride an army tank during the revolution. The Army's support for the revolution was crucial: only it was strong enough to take on and defeat the Securitate.

Anger Erupts

The crowd at the rally was angry: people knew about Timisoara and about the other East European revolutions. As a large group of workers and students began shouting "Killer!" and "Timisoara!," others joined in and began booing. Shocked, Ceausescu stopped talking. The TV station, probably afraid to transmit the dictator's embarrassment, cut transmission of the speech to the whole country.

This was the turning point. When transmission began again, Ceausescu was talking. But it was too late: the whole country had seen Ceausescu silenced by the crowd.

Below *Nicolai Ceausescu in the middle of a six-hour address to the Romanian Communist Party's fourteenth Congress on November 20, 1989. Delegates gave him more than 60 standing ovations as he condemned the changes sweeping other countries in Eastern Europe and restated Romania's commitment to resist reform. One month and five days later he was dead.*

THE DICTATORSHIP OF NICOLAI CEAUSESCU

Nicolai Ceausescu was a brutal dictator. The Securitate (secret police) had almost 100,000 full-time members. One-third of the people were said to be informers. People, sometimes even foreign travelers, vanished without trace in the hands of the Securitate.

Ordinary Romanians lived in desperate poverty. In the province of Transylvania, people were rationed to five eggs, two pounds of flour, two pounds of sugar, and two pounds of cheese per month. Meanwhile Nicolai Ceausescu and his wife Elena lived in great wealth. Even their Labrador dogs were driven around Bucharest in their own limousine.

Right *The swimming pool in the Ceausescus' private villa, Romania Sinaia. Ceausescu lived in a world almost totally cut off from that of ordinary Romanians. Just before his execution he said: "I have done everything to create a decent and rich life for the people in the country, as in no other country in the world."*

At first, people just milled around the streets. There was no dissident movement to lead them. But that did not stop the regime from replying in the only way it knew how: that night troops shot and bayoneted unarmed protesters. On December 22 the people came out in huge numbers, chanting "Liberty! Democracy! Freedom!" Ceausescu, realizing the people were against him, feared for his safety and fled Bucharest.

Then the Army changed sides and declared its support for the revolution. It sensed that Ceausescu was losing power, and it wanted to be on the winning side.

Counterattack

The Securitate, in a desperate attempt to save themselves and Ceausescu, launched a counterattack that night, opening fire on the demonstrators once again. Over the next four days, hundreds of people were killed.

Above A man raises a defiant fist, and another gives a V-for-Victory sign, as Romanians drop to the ground to protect themselves from gunfire during fighting between the army and pro-Ceausescu troops in Bucharest, December 24, 1989. Hundreds were killed in fierce fighting in different towns.

Right Romanians line up for voting papers during the first free elections after the collapse of the regime. As in other Communist countries, voting was new for most people. There were accusations of vote-rigging in the Romanian elections but Western observers thought they were fair.

But the counterrevolution was defeated on Christmas Day. Nicolai Ceausescu, and his wife Elena, had been captured, and on December 25, after a short trial, they were executed by firing squad. December 27 saw the last of the fighting.

Power quickly passed into the hands of the National Salvation Front, a group formed during the revolution. The Front was run by anti-Ceausescu Communists and by army generals and bureaucrats who had switched sides during the revolution. In May 1990 the National Salvation Front was victorious in the elections.

EYEWITNESS

Andrea Donea, a young taxi driver and one of the leading revolutionaries, on the events in the Square on December 21: "Everybody's yelling and screaming, and they've all got their heads like this [he shielded his face with the lapel of his coat] because the Securitate used to film you in the Square. At that moment we had the feeling and the sensation that maybe we win. We can see they're scared, and in that moment we see we can do something and that we're really a force."

TIME LINE

1965
March: Nicolai Ceausescu becomes First Secretary of the Communist Party.

1989
December 16–17: Protest in defense of Father Laszlo Tokes in Timisoara. Demonstrations broken up by force.
December 21: Ceausescu silenced by crowd in Bucharest.
December 22: Army switches sides; Ceausescus flee; Securitate fights back; fighting continues for five days.
December 23: National Salvation Front declares itself in charge.
December 25: Nicolai and Elena Ceausescu executed by firing squad.

1990
May: National Salvation Front wins elections to Parliament; Ion Iliescu elected President.

BULGARIA

The dissident movement in Bulgaria was small and oppressed. The revolution was led by reform-minded Communists who were determined to stay in power.

A turning point came in May 1989, when members of the huge ethnic Turkish minority held a series of demonstrations to protest against the campaign, started by the hard-line Communist leader Todor Zhivkov, to destroy Turkish culture. The police response was brutal: 60 people were killed, hundreds arrested, and over 500 deported to Turkey. As Zhivkov stepped up his anti-Turk speeches, 350,000 Bulgarian Turks fled to Turkey.

In 1885, after over 500 years of occupation by the Turks, modern Bulgaria was founded with its current borders. The Russians occupied the country in 1944 and set up a largely Communist regime headed by the veteran international revolutionary, Georgi Dimitrov.

Todor Zhivkov was, in 1989, Eastern Europe's longest-serving Communist leader, having come to power in 1954. For most of his rule, he did not have to cope with a sustained level of dissent. In 1989, however, the country began to stir as people learned of events in the rest of Eastern Europe and the Soviet Union.

Zhivkov had gone too far. Western governments and organizations protested loudly, Mikhail Gorbachev refused to back his policies, and leading Bulgarian Communists began to move against Zhivkov.

Dissident Action

A second key event was an international conference on the environment, in the capital Sofia, between October 16 and November 3. As Western ecologists, diplomats, and journalists gathered, Bulgarian dissident groups, such as Ecoglasnost and the Independent Society for Human Rights, staged open-air demonstrations, circulated petitions, and talked to conference delegates.

The regime tried, again, to use violence to smash the protests. But when the Bulgarian police publicly beat up Ecoglasnost members, the international conference delegates protested, and the government was forced to back down and offer an apology.

TIME LINE

1989
May: Ethnic Turks campaign against forced assimilation.
June: Huge exodus of ethnic Turks begins.
October 16–November 3: CSCE Environment Conference in Sofia provides cover for opposition activity.
October 25: Petar Mladenov resigns
October 26: About thirty Ecoglasnost demonstrators beaten up in Sofia.
November 10: Todor Zhivkov ousted.
Fifty thousand people demonstrate for democracy in Sofia.

1990
June: Free elections. Socialist Party forms government.

A Turkish mother with her two children preparing to leave Bulgaria for Turkey. The persecution of the Turks began in 1984–85 when the government forced them to change their Islamic names and adopt Bulgarian ones. The government claimed the name-changing was voluntary.

Ecoglasnost continued its demonstrations, and on November 3 delivered a petition with 11,500 signatures to the parliament.

Meanwhile, on October 24, the leading Communist Party reformer, Foreign Minister Petar Mladenov, delivered a letter of resignation. He sensed the time was right to challenge Zhivkov. The letter accused the Party leader of establishing a regime of personal power and of "eating out of the same trough as the rotten [Romanian] dictator Ceausescu."

Petar Mladenov

There followed two weeks of behind-the-scenes maneuvering, as Mladenov secured the support of the Politburo and of Mikhail Gorbachev, for his bid to remove Zhivkov. The blow fell on November 10, when at a press conference, Prime Minister Georgi Atanasov announced Zhivkov's resignation.

A Bulgarian woman holds a portrait of new Communist Party and state leader Petar Mladenov during a pro-democracy rally in Sofia on November 10. Dissident groups were divided at first in their reactions to Mladenov: some remained opposed to Communism, while others wanted to give Mladenov a chance to implement his promised democratic reforms.

Mladenov quickly put himself at the head of the reform movement, announcing that political prisoners would be released, that the Muslim and Turkish minorities would have their rights restored, and declared that he supported free elections.

Leading opposition groups established the Union of Democratic Forces (UDF). But the UDF was neither strong enough nor popular enough to outmaneuver the Communists, and in June 1990 the Communist Party, now renamed the Socialist Party, was elected to power in the first free elections in Bulgaria since 1932.

Thousands of supporters of the Union of Democratic Forces demonstrate in front of the Bulgarian Assembly in Sofia on July 11, 1990. The protesters were dissatisfied with the election results, claiming that the Socialist Party cheated. As in Romania, though, it appears that the elections were largely free and fair.

EASTERN EUROPE SINCE 1989

The Eastern European revolutions of 1989 mark a clear turning point in world history. For over 100 years many people had believed that a Communist society would provide a fairer and free life for its citizens. Many died for this belief. But when the people of Eastern Europe overthrew their regimes in 1989, they were rejecting not just the governments in power but Communism itself. When, in 1991, the Communist system in the Soviet Union collapsed, for most people the idea that Communism would one day replace capitalism belonged to the past.

The revolutions of 1989 were unique in one fundamental respect. The French, Russian, and Chinese revolutions aimed to replace an old system with a new one. In Eastern Europe in 1989, however, the people rejected an unsuccessful and inefficient system in favor of the tried and tested economic and political system of Western Europe.

Right *Twenty-four former members of the Romanian ruling elite on trial for having worked in the Securitate. In most Eastern European countries, some former leading Communists have been tried for crimes they are said to have committed.*

Below *Boris Yeltsin addresses a crowd of supporters defending the Russian parliament—the "White House"—during the August 1991 attempt to overthrow Mikhail Gorbachev and restore hard-line Communism in the Soviet Union. The coup failed and helped bring down the Communist system and the Soviet Union itself.*

Replacing Communism

But getting rid of Communist rule in 1989 did not in itself mean that a Western-style system would be installed. To do that the Communist system has to be removed—and that is what the countries of Eastern Europe have been trying to do since 1989.

Throughout the region, free elections are established features of the political system. At the same time, new political parties have emerged and in most countries represent opinions across the political spectrum.

Throughout Eastern Europe, and in the Soviet Union after August 1991, the revolutions were followed by the tearing down of statues of Vladimir Ilyich Lenin, the first leader of Soviet Russia.

Free media—TV, radio, and the press—are an essential element of a free society, and in most Eastern European countries these are slowly emerging. The most difficult task facing the governments of Eastern Europe, however, is how to transform the old, centralized economic systems into market economies that can compete with the strong economies in the rest of the world.

Much of Eastern European industry under Communism was old-fashioned and uncompetitive. For example, many of the shipyards on the Baltic Coast in Poland, where Solidarity was born, were kept afloat by government subsidies. Such enterprises have to be closed. This has made many people unemployed, as no new businesses have opened to employ them. So some governments have continued to keep their outdated industries alive in order not to put too many people out of work. The new government of Slovakia, for instance, has not shut down its arms industry for this reason.

Disillusioned Voters

In some countries—for example, Poland and Czechoslovakia—radical economic reforms have been introduced. These have produced economic growth and have given some people a higher standard of living. But many people, particularly the old, have suffered badly and have fallen below the poverty line.

Partly because of this, voters in Eastern Europe have begun to return left-wing parties to power. Throughout the region, the euphoria people felt just after the revolutions has disappeared as they realize that Western prosperity cannot be achieved simply by overthrowing Communist regimes. On the other hand, progress has been made toward establishing democratic structures in all Eastern European countries.

The Old Town in Prague, the capital of the Czech Republic. Prague was popular with Western visitors before the Communists fell, but since 1989 it has been flooded with tourists from around the globe. The city now has a large community of young Americans and boasts its own English-language newspapers.

TIME LINE IN 1989

June 4: Solidarity victorious in Polish elections.

16: Imre Nagy reburied in Hungary.

August 24: Tadeusz Mazowiecki becomes Polish prime minister.

October 18: Erich Honecker resigns.

23: Republic Day in Hungary.

November 9: Berlin Wall opens.

10: Todor Zhivkov resigns as Communist leader in Bulgaria.

December 16–17 Protests in Timisoara, Romania.

24: Communist regime in Czechoslovakia steps down.

December 25: Nicolai and Elena Ceausescu executed in Romania.

29: Vaclav Havel elected president of Czechoslovakia.

The revolutions of 1989 ended Communist rule first in Poland and Hungary, then in East Germany, Bulgaria, Czechoslovakia, and Romania. In seven short months the political map of Europe had been redrawn. The speed at which events took place left Western governments astonished and surprised: overnight they had to learn how to deal not with possible enemies in the East—the Communist regimes—but with friends.

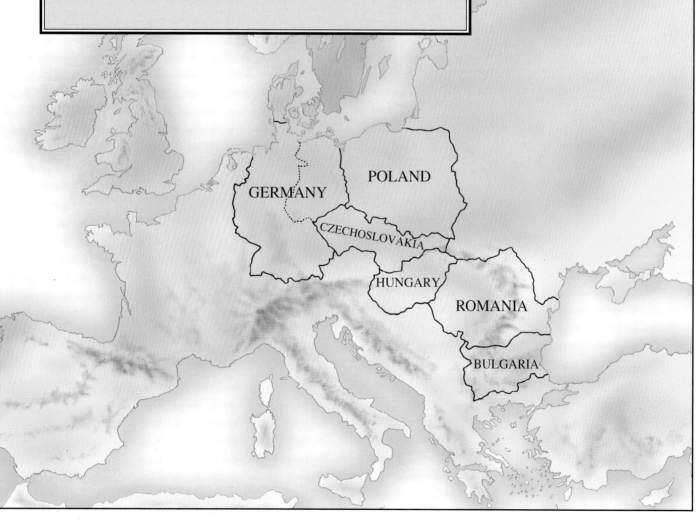

GLOSSARY

Bloc A group of countries or political parties that has come together to promote a particular interest.

Capitalism An economic and political system in which property is privately owned, there is a free market, and most people work for private employers.

Coalition A union or alliance (particularly of political parties or states).

Cold War The state of strained relations between the United States (and other Western countries) and the Soviet Union (and other East European countries) that lasted from 1945 to 1989.

Communism The idea that all property should be held in common and private wealth abolished. In practice it has been a system of government under which industry and commerce are controlled by the state.

Counterrevolution An attempt to overthrow a revolution.

Democracy A political system in which political power is—at least in theory—in the hands of the whole adult population.

Dictatorship A form of government in which one person has sole and complete political power.

Dissident Someone who strongly opposes the policies of a government or political party.

Human rights The rights that all people hold because they are human and that may not be forbidden to them by any government.

Imperial Russia The Russian Empire, which lasted from the 17th century to the 20th century. It was overthrown by the Russian Revolution of 1917.

Market economy The economic system in which all or most enterprises are owned privately and the forces of supply and demand are not obstructed by government interference.

Multi-party democracy A democracy in which two or more political parties compete with each other for power.

Nationalism The belief that one group of people forms a natural community, should have its own political system, and should be independent of others.

Politburo The most powerful decision-making body in a Communist Party.

Prussia A powerful German kingdom in the eighteenth and nineteenth centuries. It was the most important state in the Second German Empire of 1871–1918.

Revolution The overthrow of a political or social system.

Satellite party In Communist countries, a political party that appeared to be independent but was in fact under the control of the Communist Party.

Socialism In Communist countries, this word was often used instead of Communism.

Stalinism The most brutal form of Communist government, so called after the bloody and ruthless Soviet leader Joseph Stalin who ruled the Soviet Union from the mid-1920s to 1953.

Strike Work stoppage by a group of workers in a business, factory, etc., to protest low wages or bad working conditions. In a general strike, all workers in one country strike.

Warsaw Pact Properly known as the Warsaw Treaty Organization, the Warsaw Pact (founded in 1955) was a military alliance of the countries of Eastern Europe. Its members were Albania (until 1968), Czechoslovakia, East Germany, Hungary, Poland, Romania, and the Soviet Union. The Warsaw Pact dissolved in 1991.

Welfare state The system whereby the state uses money raised by taxes to provide services for the whole of society. These services may be unemployment benefits, cheap housing, a health service, or an education system.

World War II The second great European war in this century, it lasted from 1939 to 1945. It was fought between the Axis powers (Germany, Italy, and Japan) and the Allies (the United States, the Soviet Union, Great Britain, France, Australia, New Zealand, and others). In 1945 Germany and Japan were defeated and Europe was divided.

FURTHER INFORMATION

BOOKS

Bulgaria in Pictures. Minneapolis: Lerner Publications, 1994.

Clark, Mary Jane Behrends. *The Commonwealth of Independent States.* Headliners. Brookfield, CT: Millbrook Press, 1992.

Cross, Robin. *Aftermath of War.* World War II. New York: Thomson Learning, 1994.

Eastern Europe: Opposing Viewpoints. San Diego: Greenhaven, 1990.

Gilbert, Adrian. *The Russian Revolution.* Revolution! New York: Thomson Learning, 1996.

Hawkes, N. *Glasnost and Perestroika.* World Issues. Vero Beach, FL: Rourke Publishing, 1990.

Kort, Michael. *The Cold War.* Brookfield, CT: Millbrook Press, 1994.

Kort, Michael. *The Rise and Fall of the Soviet Union.* New York: Franklin Watts, 1992.

Mirable, Lisa. *The Berlin Wall.* Turning Points in World History. New York: Silver Burdett Press, 1991.

The New World Order: Opposing Viewpoints. San Diego: Greenhaven, 1991.

Poland in Pictures. Minneapolis: Lerner Publications, 1994.

Steins, Richard. *The Postwar Years: The Cold War and the Atomic Age (1950-1959).* First Person America. New York: Twenty-First Century Books, 1993.

Streussguth, Thomas. *Soviet Leaders from Lenin to Gorbachev.* Minneapolis: The Oliver Press, 1992.

For older readers

Fischer, Tibor. *Under the Frog.* New York: The New Press, 1992. A dark comic novel set in Hungary in the years before the revolution of 1956.

Glenny, Misha. *The Rebirth of History: Eastern Europe in the Age of Democracy.* New York: Penguin 1991. An examination of developments after the revolutions.

MOVIES

Movies were among the main forms of expressing opposition to Communism. East European movies are not often shown, and only a few are available on videotape. Among those worth looking for are films by Andrzej Wajda (*Man of Marble* [1977] and *Man of Iron* [1980], and *Danton* [1983], in which Danton stands for Lech Walesa and Robespierre stands for Jaruzelski).

INDEX